We Walk by Faith

WE WALK

BY

FAITH

*Stories from Britain,
Europe, Cape Verde,
and the Middle East*

by

Helen Temple

NAZARENE PUBLISHING HOUSE
Kansas City, Missouri

ISBN: 0-8341-0617-5

Printed in the
United States of America

CONTENTS

PREFACE

The stories this year are about Nazarenes in Britain, Cape Verde, Europe, and the Middle East. Though no theme was specified, they are all about people who have gone through fiery trials, and learned to walk victoriously by faith.

As in other years, the basic facts in these stories are true. Where some information was lacking, we have tried to portray how it might have happened. Conversation and details of description have been added to make the stories seem more real to the readers.

These are real people who are still living. They will be grateful for your prayers as they continue to work for God, sometimes in very difficult places.

As you read of their lives, may God help us to learn from their heroic examples that we can all be victorious if we walk by faith.

I am especially grateful to Mrs. Samuel Krikorian and Mr. Percy Davies who shared their life stories with me. And to Mrs. Thomas Long, Mrs. Earl Mosteller, and Rev. Earl Morgan who gave us the inspiring stories of ordinary Christians made extraordinary by the grace of God.

—Helen Temple

SET FREE

Carmellina pulled the covers higher to shut out the brightness of the sun streaming through the window. Weakness engulfed her. She felt she could not even lift her hand to her face.

She could hear her husband, Domenico, rattling dishes as he fixed hot milk and bread for himself and their teenage children. Then with a rush of footsteps and laughter they were all out of the house and gone and she was alone.

She sighed and turned her face to the wall. Tears of exasperation trickled from the corners of her eyes onto the pillow.

Oh, why can't I die! she thought desperately. I'm no use to my children. I'm a disgrace to my husband. They would be better off if I were dead.

She could hear the neighbor women calling cheerful greetings to each other as they scrubbed their front steps and swept the sidewalks. How long had it been since she had done those things? She could not remember. This terrible depression and weakness seemed to have had her in its grip forever.

The front door creaked on its hinges. That would be one of her good neighbors, coming in to clean her house and wash the dishes and the clothes, doing the things that she ought to be doing.

She lay still, more depressed with every sound of her neighbor's energetic sweeping, scrubbing, and dusting.

Had she ever been happy and industrious like that? Carmellina wondered. She could scarcely remember a time. Even when she was in her teens, she had been sad. Often she had sat at her window at night looking up at the stars and the moon and longing for something or someone that would give meaning to life.

"Signora," her neighbor said softly, after awhile. "Signora, are you awake?"

"Yes," Carmellina said in a weak voice, without moving.

The neighbor sat down on the edge of the bed and put her hand on Carmellina's forehead. "You are too cool," she said. "It is from weakness. I don't think you are eating. Can you sit up against the pillows and eat some hot soup?"

Carmellina shook her head. "I'm not hungry," she said.

"Even so, you must eat, or you will never get strong," her neighbor said cheerfully. She propped Carmellina up in bed with extra pillows, and brought her a bowl of hot chicken soup. "Eat this," she commanded, holding out a spoonful.

Carmellina opened her mouth and took it like a child, too ashamed of her helplessness to refuse. After a dozen spoonfuls she turned her head away. "I can't swallow any more," she said.

"Carmellina, you need to see a doctor," her neighbor said.

"It's no use," Carmellina answered. "I've been to doctors and doctors. I've been to psychologists. None of them have helped me."

"Have you talked to the priest?"

8

"Yes. Many times. And to priests in other churches, too. None have helped. I wish I could die."

"Ah, but death is in the Lord's hands," her neighbor said briskly. "He will decide when that is to be. Until then, you need to find strength to live. Now go ahead and rest. I'll take your washing home and do it with mine. And don't worry. You'll be better one of these days, and then you can do the same for someone else."

Carmellina lay back and closed her eyes. She heard her neighbor gathering up the clothes, humming as she worked. Then the door closed and it was quiet.

She cried a little in self-pity and discouragement, and fell asleep.

Toward evening, Carmellina made herself get up and dress. Domenico would soon be coming from work. She must try to do better for his sake, poor man.

When she went to the inner courtyard to start a fire and cook supper, she found a kettle of soup simmering there on the stove, left by some kind neighbor.

The girls set the table and put bowls of soup on for everyone. They chattered about their day, directing their remarks to Domenico, as Carmellina ate in weary silence. After a few minutes she excused herself and went to lie down.

How long must she go on like this? she wondered. For months now the neighbors had been doing her housework and cooking for her family. They were wonderful friends, but they could not keep doing this. It was not right. She had to get over this somehow.

But thinking about it did not change anything. When she awakened the next morning she was still weak and still deeply depressed.

She heard her husband and the children leave, and lay in bed trying to force herself to get up.

Again the door opened and her neighbor came in. She

greeted Carmellina with a cheery good morning, and set about cleaning the house.

When she was finished she came over and stood by Carmellina's bed. "How are you this morning?" she asked.

"Just the same," Carmellina said weakly, as tears slid down her cheeks.

"I think you stay in this house alone too much," the neighbor said kindly. "You need to get out in the sunshine and see people, talk to someone. It would make you feel better."

"I know it," Carmellina said. "But I don't have any strength."

"And you never will have if you stay in that bed," the neighbor said. "Try getting up and sitting in a chair. Walk into the courtyard. When you get a little strength walk to the park. Talk to people. Come over and sit on my steps with me. It will help you."

Carmellina nodded. "I know you're right," she said, "but I just can't do it."

"Try it. Just a little at a time. You'll see, it will make you feel better," her neighbor said patting her hand. "Now I have to go. I'll look in on you tomorrow."

When she had gone, Carmellina raised herself on her elbows, then pushed herself to a sitting position on the bed, letting her legs dangle. They felt like limp rubber. She was dizzy and trembling from the exertion, but she made herself stand up and walk to a chair and sit. Through the window she could see the neighbors chatting as they scrubbed their steps.

Oh, how I wish I could do that again! she thought. She made herself a cup of strong, hot tea and drank it. Then she walked around the little courtyard. She did feel a little stronger, she admitted to herself. Perhaps a little later, she might even walk to the park, two blocks away.

In the afternoon she warmed up some of the left-over

soup and ate it. Then she dressed and set out. Her knees were shaky, but she walked the short distance to the park and sat down on a bench. It was wonderful to be out in the sunshine and the warm air. It was good to watch little children at play while their mothers talked.

My neighbor was right, she thought. I've been alone too much. It is good for me to get out.

Her head began to ache from weariness and in a panic she got up and started back, fearful that she would collapse before she got home.

She reached her house and dropped down on the bed. When she wakened from a nap she felt refreshed and better than she had for days.

That night as she lay in bed after the others were asleep, she thought about what she had done. Maybe what I need is to get a job somewhere, she thought. A job where I had to get out every day, no matter how I felt. We could certainly use the money. The more she thought about it, the more daring she felt. I'll do it, she decided. I'll do it tomorrow.

She stayed in bed until the others had gone to school or work. Then she got up and dressed, drank some hot tea and ate a bun. She looked longingly at the bed. Maybe she was being foolish. She still felt very weak. Could she keep a job if she was lucky enough to find one? She sank down on the chair and closed her eyes. I can't do it, she thought, miserably. I just can't do it. It's no use.

No—I will do it, she said to herself. I've got to try. She got up, made herself walk out the door and lock it behind her. Then she walked down the street to the corner and got on the bus going toward the center of town.

As she sank down on the seat, waves of exhaustion washed over her. Oh, I mustn't faint, she thought, closing her eyes in panic. "If You are there, God, please help me," she pleaded. "Whatever I must do to find peace, show me.

11

I can't live like this any longer."

Suddenly she was aware that calmness and strength were flowing over her from her head to her feet. She sat in silent amazement, feeling the healing strength stealing through her body. She was renewed, she was strong, she was happy!

She wanted to shout from the windows, to laugh, to clap her hands and dance in the aisle. "I'm well! I'm well!" she thought. "Thank You, Lord. Oh, thank You, Lord!"

She got off the bus at the next stop and caught another bus back home. There she changed her clothes and began to clean and scrub and polish her little house. She washed the clothes, ironed, mended, and then began cooking Domenico's favorite dinner.

The girls came home first, laughing and talking together with their friends. She could hear them outside, and realized they were delaying coming in as long as they could. My poor children, she thought. What have I done to them?

When they finally opened the door they started to whisper, tiptoeing softly into the room. They looked at the empty bed neatly made, and their eyes flew to the courtyard where Carmellina stood stirring the kettle over the fire.

"Mama!" they cried and ran to hug her. "You're better! Are you? Really?"

"Yes, I'm better," Carmellina said, hugging them tight. "The good God has made me well again."

The girls looked around at the shining house and sniffed the good food cooking. "Oh, Mama!" they cried in delight and rushed to the door to tell their friends.

When Domenico came home Carmellina was setting the table. She turned to greet him and saw the deep lines of sadness and weariness etched in his face.

"Ah, my Domenico," she said sympathetically, "come in and sit down. You look so tired. Let me bring you a cup of tea."

He stared at her. "Carmellina!" he said finally. "You —are you better?"

Her radiant face answered before she spoke. "I'm well, thank God!" she said. "He healed me on the bus this morning. It is wonderful."

"On the bus?" he said bewildered. "But I left you ill in bed."

"I know, I know," she said laughing and patting his cheek. "Come and sit down. Supper is all ready. As soon as it is on the table we will eat and I'll tell you all about it."

She was almost afraid to go to bed that night, lest she wake in the morning with the old depression and weakness. But she slept like a child and wakened at dawn full of energy and happiness. She slipped from bed and began to sweep and dust her house. What a joy it was to feel alive again!

She was scrubbing her living room floor when her neighbor came to the door and started to come in as usual. She stopped on the threshold. "Carmellina!" she exclaimed. "It's true, then! You are well again. Oh, thanks be to God! The girls said so last night, but I thought they must be mistaken. Tell me, how did it happen?"

Carmellina sat back on her heels in the middle of the floor and told her friend how she had started out to find work, in hopes it would help her; and how she had nearly fainted on the bus, and had cried out in anguish to God, and He had made her well, instantly.

The word spread up and down the street, and one after another, the women who had been helping Carmellina came by to see for themselves.

Every morning that week Carmelina woke up at 5:30

wondering if she still had her new strength and joy; and every morning she thrilled to the vitality that filled her whole being.

On Sunday morning she decided she must go to God's house somewhere and give public thanks to God for what He had done. She knew that in the church her brother-in-law attended, people often stood up and gave thanks to God for blessings.

I will go there, she decided.

She walked into the service just as it was beginning. Those who knew her gasped when they saw her radiant, happy face.

When the singing ended, Carmellina stood to her feet. "May I say something this morning?" she asked.

"Of course," the missionary pastor said.

"My friends," Carmellina said, "some of you know that I have been searching for something to give meaning to my life for years. You know how I've suffered from terrible depression and weakness. I've been to psychologists and doctors. I've counselled with priests. I've followed the advice of my friends, but nothing helped. I haven't been able to care for my family and my good neighbors have cleaned my house and washed my clothes and cooked for my family, to my shame.

"Last week, in desperation, I decided to go to the city and look for work. I thought if I got out of the house and had something I had to do it might help me. When I got on the bus, I nearly fainted with exhaustion. I was terrified. What if I should die there among strangers? I cried out to God and said, 'If You are there, God, please help me. Whatever I must do to find peace and joy, show me, for I cannot live like this any longer.' And do you know, my friends, for the first time in my 55 years, I met il Signore" (the Lord). Her voice rose to a shout: "I have met the Lord! Do you hear? He has come into my life and has changed

14

me! He has given me peace and joy. The depression is gone!"

Tears of joy flowed down her cheeks. "That was Tuesday morning," she continued. "Wednesday, Thursday, Friday, and Saturday I awoke very early, afraid that He, my new Friend, would not be there. But praise God, I'm here this morning in church to tell all of you, my brothers and sisters, that He didn't leave me, and He's here with me this morning!"

Shouts of "Amen!" "Praise God!" and "Alleluia!" rose from all over the church hall. Men blew heartily into their handkerchiefs, and the ladies on the other side of the church wiped their eyes. The missionary and his wife wept too and thanked God that they had been privileged to be in Sicily that morning to hear this new Christian's testimony of deliverance.

The next week the missionary and his wife arranged to call on Carmellina at her home. When they arrived, she invited them into her living room. It was sparkling from her recent scrubbing.

"Please be seated," Carmellina said. "I'll prepare some tea."

She went to the courtyard and put the kettle on the stove. While she waited for it to boil she began to bring in straightbacked, wooden chairs and put them in a circle around her visitors. There were 10 in all. Then she excused herself and slipped out the front door.

The missionaries looked at each other mystified. They had visited in many homes in Sicily, but this was the first time anything like this had happened.

In a moment Carmellina returned and excused herself again to finish preparing the tea.

Soon there was a knock at the door. An elderly lady let herself in. She greeted the missionary wife with a kiss and the husband with a handshake and sat down next to the wife. Soon there was another knock and a young woman with two tiny children came in, greeted them, and sat down with a child on each knee. Then there came a middle-aged lady with her six-year-old son. She too greeted them, and sat down in the circle. One after another 10 ladies came in, each one greeting the missionaries like old and dear friends.

Then Carmellina came in carrying a beautiful hand-decorated tray on which were 13 tea cups, a huge pot of tea, and a sugar bowl.

She served her guests and as all began sipping the hot tea she said, "Pastore, these ladies are my dear neighbors who remember when I was so ill. These are the ladies who cleaned my house when I was so depressed I couldn't leave my bed. They cooked for my family and did my shopping, and they listened to me sympathetically when I cried and agonized over my state. They have seen in these few days that I am a new and different woman. And now, Pastore, they are here to listen while you talk about the Lord."

There on that bright, sunny November morning as the missionaries shared God's Word with Carmellina's neighbors, the Ladies' Bible Study was born—the first Nazarene Bible study for ladies in Sicily.

Carmellina asked many questions about the Spirit-filled life. She had had very little schooling as a child, but she was an eager pupil of the Holy Spirit and her spiritual insights constantly amazed the missionaries.

About six weeks after Carmellina had met the Lord on the bus, she again stood to her feet in church to testify. Ordinarily Carmellina's testimony was given with a flashing smile and a triumphant note that blessed everyone. Today she seemed sober and restrained.

"My dear brothers and sisters," she said softly. "I have a confession to make this morning. I am a woman with four children and two grandchildren, and . . . and . . ."

16

she hesitated, then went on—"the man I have been living with for 25 years, the father of my children, is not legally my husband.

"But glory to God, Alleluia, His blessed Holy Spirit has been talking to me and now I want to be married! I want a beautiful church wedding with flowers and all."

Again the church rang with shouts of "Amen," "Praise the Lord" and "Alleluia."

Carmellina's situation was not unusual among unbelievers in Sicily. The complications and legalities and the expense involved in having a church marriage were so great that many just ignored it all and simply began living together.

Tears flowed that morning even from the eyes of some very proper professional people who were not easily stirred. Domenico's brother shouted "Gloria a Dio!" All felt they were enjoying a taste of heaven, as the sense of the approval and blessing of God filled the room.

"We'll have a beautiful church wedding for Carmellina, won't we?" the missionary wife asked her husband after the service that morning.

"I don't know, dear," he said. "These things take time and the legal red tape is endless. She can just go to the city hall and have a civil ceremony and everything will be fine."

But Carmellina and the missionary wife were much more determined to do it the way she wanted.

"I really wanted to be married right away when I knew it was God's will," Carmellina said, "but my married daughter said 'Mother you've waited 25 years. What's the hurry now? Let's wait till winter is over and have the wedding in April.'"

And so on the beautiful sunny spring morning of April 30, 1977, Carmellina and Domenico Puglisi were united in holy matrimony at the Nazarene Church, after first having

17

the civil ceremony at the Comune, as the law required.

More than 100 people came to their wedding. Half of them were Roman Catholic friends and relatives of Carmellina and for most of them it was their first time in a Protestant service.

At the close of the very sacred ceremony, Carmellina asked the congregation to sing her favorite hymn, "Holy Brothers, Forward We Go!" She sang the last chorus as a solo, and with her radiant face turned heavenward she shouted the last phrase, "In the holy name of Jesus!"

The congregation applauded enthusiastically, including Domenico, though he himself was not converted yet.

The next Sunday morning, Carmellina was in church, smiling and quickly on her feet to testify. "I feel like a brand-new bride," she said, and a wave of friendly understanding laughter rippled over the congregation. She went on with a fervent testimony of praise and thanksgiving to her Savior that brought a holy hush upon the waiting people.

She was indeed a brand-new woman in the Lord. She grew in grace like a flower in a watered garden. She joined the church and attended the district assembly as an elected delegate. It was her first time ever to leave the island of Sicily.

Carmellina was a gifted leader, who soon held many positions of service in the church. At the district assembly in 1978, Carmellina was a delegate again and took her second son, Alfio with her. He attended every session and seemed deeply impressed.

When the assembly was over and they returned home, Carmellina was awakened in the night by Alfio.

"Mama, I can't sleep," he said. "My heart is full of distress."

She was instantly awake. "You need the Lord," she said. "Let's pray."

That night Alfio accepted Christ, and on Sunday morning he was in church with Carmellina to tell about it.

That summer the missionary held a baptismal service for Carmellina and four other new Christians. One of them was Carmellina's friend, won to Christ through her morning Bible study.

One by one Carmellina was bringing in her sheaves to Christ.

Others have been influenced for good by her ministry. Some have accepted Christ and joined the Church of the Nazarene. Others have received salvation but for family reasons have not felt able to join yet. This does not discourage Carmellina.

"It will come," she says confidently. "It will come. If we just keep them following Christ and being obedient to the Holy Spirit, it will come. I'm not anxious. Let the Lord lead."

When Carmellina was elected to the church board in Catania last year, the first woman ever elected to the board in that church, it was a significant tribute to the respect and honor in which the Catania Nazarenes hold Carmellina. And rightly so, for she is one of God's choice people.

ONE MORE TIME

A sharp rap at the door roused the Cape Verde missionary from the book he was reading as he sat by the window, trying to catch a little of the night breeze from the sea.

He was a little surprised at the knock. It was already dark outside, with no moon, and Cape Verdians did not travel about a lot at night.

He went to the door and opened it. "Yes?" he said into the darkness.

"Senhor," a pleading voice said. "Can we go over to the church tower room and pray just one more time?"

The anticipated enjoyment of an evening at home evaporated.

"Of course, Senhor Humberto," he said warmly. He picked up his flashlight and joined the man waiting outside.

Humberto had not been a Christian very long, but from the night he accepted Christ, he had prayed earnestly for his estranged wife Idalina, now living on another island with their little daughter, Maria Celeste. He had not seen his daughter since she was a baby. He could scarcely remember what it had felt like to hold the tiny mite in his arms.

Tonight the missionary and the burdened husband and father climbed the dark narrow stairs to the tower room as they had done many times before. The tower had become Humberto's special place of prayer when his faith could not quite master his problems alone.

They prayed aloud, sometimes together, sometimes separately, agonizing over the estranged wife. They prayed silently, each wrestling with the problem in his own way.

The devil slipped into the prayer meeting, pointing out how hopeless it was; chiding Humberto for clinging to his Christian faith, assuring him it would cost him his wife, and urging him to give it up.

Give it up? That was the devil's undoing. The memories of that night when God had come and wiped his record clear and filled his life with peace came flooding back. Never could he give up the fellowship he had found with Christ. Not even for Idalina whom he loved almost better than his own life. No, not even for her. If she could just once know the joy that he had found, he knew she would want to come back. That was his burden and his hope.

Humberto had written to her right after he was saved. He had told her he was a different man, and begged her to come back home. His letters were never answered.

How many times had he come to this tower in the night to pray for her? More than he could remember. Yet tonight, as before, he could not point to one shred of evidence that God was doing anything about Idalina.

He lifted his tear-stained face in the darkness and said, "Senhor, do you think God can save Idalina? Is she beyond His reach?"

"Senhor Humberto," the missionary answered, "God won't make Idalina come to Him against her will. But He has a thousand ways to help Idalina change her mind about that. I believe she will be saved someday. We must

21

believe God and keep praying the obstacles away. God loves Idalina, Humberto."

"I know He does," Humberto said. "I know His love. He found me, a proud, ambitious man as I was, and brought me to the foot of His cross. I know how He loves. But it's been such a long time we've prayed and there has been no answer. Not even a glimmer of a sign that He is getting to her. The burden gets so heavy . . ." a sob choked off his words. He brushed the tears away brusquely. "Sometimes it's hard to keep believing," he said. "Then I come and ask you to pray with me. Thank you, Senhor. Thank you for always being willing to come to the tower with me when the load gets too heavy."

He reached out and grasped the missionary's hand with feelings too deep to express.

It was not the last time that the missionary answered a knock at his door in the night and heard that plea for "just one more time" of prayer in the tower. Many nights he and Humberto battled through the discouragement and loneliness to new courage and faith in that little upper room. But the years slipped past and there still was no sign that God had been able to touch Idalina.

When the mission council voted for these missionaries to move to the island of St. Vicente and open new work there, the missionaries were almost afraid to break the news to Humberto. How would he feel, knowing that his prayer partner over these hard years was moving away? Would he be able to carry his burden alone?

The missionary waited until they were sharing a time of fellowship together one evening and then he said "Humberto, did you know that the mission council wants to open work on the island of St. Vicente?"

"Yes," Humberto said. "I've heard. I'm delighted. Idalina lives on St. Vicente, you know. This may be the first sign that God is answering our prayers."

"The council has asked my wife and me to be the ones to move to St. Vicente to open this new work," the missionary said, watching Humberto closely.

For a fleeting moment, sharp disappointment showed on Humberto's face, quickly erased by joy. "Ah, Senhor!" he cried. "You care! You can find a way to reach Idalina. Oh, Senhor, this is of the Lord. I'll pray. I'll go to the tower alone, but I shall feel you are praying with me. Together we'll storm heaven until even Idalina's stony heart will be melted. And you will be there to lead her to the Lord. Praise God!"

Inwardly the missionary was not quite as confident as Humberto that his going to St. Vicente would result in Idalina's salvation, but he determined that he would do his best to see this happen.

As soon as the missionary family was settled in a home on St. Vicente, they began calling throughout the community around them. And among their contacts was Idalina.

She was a pretty woman, sparkling and intelligent. She greeted the missionary graciously when he called at her door. When he told her who he was and invited her to church, her welcoming smile vanished. "Thank you, Senhor," she said in a cool, distant voice, "I'm not interested in your religion."

"Could my wife and daughters come by and take your little girl to Sunday school perhaps?" he asked, trying to keep a thread for further contact.

"No, thank you, Senhor," she said. "We just don't care for your religion."

"We will be holding our Sunday school and church in a rented hall just around the corner from your home," the missionary persisted, holding out his card.

She ignored his outstretched hand and said with a tinge of irritation in her voice, "Really, Senhor, I am a spiritualist. I conduct séances. You would not expect me to come to your services, would you?"

She was closing the door as she spoke, and the missionary had time only to say, "Good day."

But he went back. Sometimes he took his daughters. Sometimes his wife went with him. His older daughter became a close friend of Maria Celeste.

Most of the time the missionaries did not pressure Idalina with invitations to church. They worked first to become friends. When Idalina no longer felt threatened, she began to respond to their friendship. After a time she let Maria Celeste go to the missionary's home to play with their children. It was really a convenience while she was at work to know that the child was in a safe place.

Marie Celeste was a beautiful little girl, and even at the age of 11, she had a sweet singing voice.

At first she invited the missionary's daughters to come to the beach with her on Sundays. When she discovered that they would not go on Sunday, she began going to Sunday school with them.

In a few months, Maria Celeste accepted Christ as her Savior. She was at the missionary's home even oftener after that, so much, indeed, that she was like another daughter to them. The smallest missionary child, a little more than three, thought her favorite Sunday school song "Brilho Celeste" ("Heavenly Sunshine") was about her new friend and went around the house singing "Maria Celeste."

Maria loved the songs she learned in Sunday school and at the missionary's home. She sang them often, in church and in her own home. Many of the songs had been translated by her father, whom she did not remember.

In all the months that the missionaries had been cultivating Idalina's friendship, she had remained polite, friendly, and totally disinterested in their faith. It began to look as though it was hopeless to try to reach this cultured, refined, self-assured woman.

Then one afternoon there was a knock at the missionary's door. When they opened it, they were startled to see Idalina. She had never come to their home unless they invited her, before.

"Come in Idalina," they said warmly.

She came in nervously, and sat down in the chair they offered.

"Oh, dear God, don't let her tell us that Maria Celeste can't come here any more," the missionary's wife prayed, as she saw Idalina's agitation.

"I want to pray," Idalina said abruptly. "I want to know your God."

What joy! They knelt in relief and delight and there in the living room as they prayed together, Idalina met Jesus.

"Can we tell my husband?" she asked through her tears as she rose from her knees.

"I'll go to the telegraph office now and send him the good news," the missionary said.

The answer came swiftly back. "Coming on the first boat."

It seemed an interminable time before the tiny sailboat appeared on the horizon a few days later. The missionary met Humberto at the dock. His wife went to get Idalina and Maria Celeste. There in the missionary's living room Humberto and Idalina had a beautiful reconciliation, as their 12-year-old daughter watched in delight, gazing at the father she was meeting for the first time.

There had to be a second honeymoon, and it had to include Maria Celeste. They could not go far, for it was only two hours from one coast of the island to the other. But the happy family borrowed the missionary's jeep and went away for a few days to rebuild their lives together.

They returned to pack up Idalina's household goods and then the reunited family moved to Brava, where Humberto was now governor of the island.

Maria Celeste did not stay in Brava very long. The only high school in the islands was on St. Vicente. She returned to the island in a few weeks to complete her schooling and she and her beloved missionary friends were reunited again.

One day, much later, Humberto gave up his government position to become director of publishing for the Church of the Nazarene on St. Vicente. The salary was much less than he had earned in the government office, but he felt keenly the need for Christian literature for Cape Verde, and he believed God was directing him to make the move.

Idalina became NWMS president in the church she once had refused to attend. Humberto became Sunday school superintendent. And Maria Celeste graduated from high school and went to Portugal to study in the University of Coimbra, while she lived with Christian friends.

The missionary family was not in St. Vicente to see all of these developments, for the Department of World Mission asked them to go to Brazil and open the Church of the Nazarene there.

It was very hard to leave Cape Verde. It was hard to leave the church in St. Vicente and their good friends of many years. It took some praying to be sure this was God's will to tear up their roots from this place they loved and move on to a different culture in a new nation.

There were hard days and joyous days in the new country. There were burdened days and rejoicing days as the church was planted and began to grow. Every few years the missionaries went back to the United States for furlough, and then returned to Brazil.

On one of these furloughs in 1970, the missionaries

went to Great Britain for a tour of the churches on their way back to Brazil. Their boat was scheduled to stop in Lisbon, Portugal. They wrote to their old friends from Cape Verde who had moved to Lisbon and told them. When the boat docked there were their Cape Verdian friends waiting to greet them. Eagerly they exchanged greetings and hugs, and asked about their many good friends on the islands; and especially about Humberto and Idalina.

"Idalina is in the hospital here in Lisbon," the Cape Verdian friends said. "She's just had surgery. Could you take time to come and see her?"

The missionaries checked. Yes, there was just time to make a quick visit.

What a surprise it was when they walked into Idalina's hospital room! Tears of gladness streamed down her cheeks as she held out her hands to them.

"Humberto has gone to heaven," she said. "Did you know? He worked so hard to finish the Portuguese translation of the hymnal *Devotion and Praise*. It was his love. His heart was very bad. And his poor hands were so crippled and swollen from arthritis he couldn't hold a pen. He had me tie the pen to his hand so that he could write. But he did it. He finished the hymnal and presented it to the district assembly. It was as though he had lived just for that. He failed very quickly afterward and in two months he went home to be with Jesus."

She dried her tears and smiled.

"And what about Maria Celeste?" the missionaries asked.

"Maria Celeste graduated from the university and took a position teaching. She has just recently married a young preacher from the seminary. They are pastoring a church. She is very busy. She's the district Christian Life chairman too."

27

The missionaries' eyes were not dry either, as they listened to the wonderful reports from those they had loved and prayed with for so long.

Reluctantly they said good-by and returned to their boat and their work in Brazil.

Three years later, the missionaries again landed in Lisbon, Portugal, this time as residents. The church had asked them to move to Portugal and open the Church of the Nazarene there. It was not hard to accept this assignment. Old friends from Cape Verde were already living there. It was almost like going home. They wrote to some and told them they were coming. A small group was at the airport to welcome them when they arrived.

Again there were hugs and handshakes and tears and much laughter as old friends were reunited. Among those at the airport were a young man and a beautiful young woman with a little boy and girl. The missionaries glanced at them frequently wondering just who they could be.

At last the young man stepped closer. "Don't you know me?" he asked. "I was in the last group you baptized in Cape Verde before you went to Brazil 15 years ago. I was only 14 then. Perhaps you don't remember me. But I'm sure you know my wife, Maria Celeste, your daughter's playmate and friend in St. Vicente. And these are our children, John and Ruth. We're visiting my mother-in-law, Idalina. She lives in Lisbon now."

"Maria Celeste!" The missionaries looked at the beautiful young woman before them. "What a lovely lady you have become! How wonderfully God has led you! Come back to Lisbon often. Our home will always be your home whenever you come."

"We'll come when we can," they promised, and in a few days went back to Cape Verde.

But not for long. Just a few months later, Maria Celeste and her husband, Jose Delgado, returned to Lisbon to stay. In 1976 they became the full-time pastors of the Church of the Nazarene in Lisbon—the first organized Church of the Nazarene in Portugal. Maria Celeste teaches junior high school during the week, and a Sunday school class on Sunday. Her voice is as beautiful as ever. She is a busy and happy mother of four children, all growing up in the church.

The Christian family with whom Maria lived when she went to the university in Coimbra are Nazarenes too, and their daughter and son-in-law are students at the European Nazarene Bible College in Busingen, Germany.

What rich dividends have come from the missionary's faithful sharing with Humberto when he came with his burdens pleading to pray in the church tower "just one more time."

JUST TO BELONG

"Mama!" seven year old Percy called, standing at the kitchen door. "Mama? Where are you?"

He stepped inside, crossed the kitchen to the sitting room and stopped at the foot of the stairs. From above he heard the murmur of someone talking. He clumped up the wooden steps to the two bedrooms above and stopped short as he saw his father kneeling beside the bed, praying.

Softly Percy backed out and tiptoed down the stairs. He scarcely breathed until he was outside the house. In his small boy's heart he felt that he had intruded on holy ground.

He stood on the doorstep thinking about what he had just seen. How did a person talk to God? he wondered. Did God really come down and listen to Papa when he talked to Him? It was a little scary to think that God might be right upstairs in Papa's bedroom.

He looked across the sunny fields toward the willows along the canal. Beyond the canal were other fields, and in the distance the River Dee, flowing at the foot of the low mountains. He could see some of his playmates hiking toward the canal. They waved and shouted at him, and he ran to join them, feeling oddly relieved to be doing something old and familiar, in place of the strange new thoughts he had been thinking.

The little village of Cefn Mawr in North Wales was scarcely more than a cluster of company-owned houses, most of them quite old, surrounding the coal mine which was the village's only reason for existence at all. Around the village on all sides were open fields, small streams, and in the distance the forested mountains. It was a paradise for children in summer. They hiked, fished, swam, and played in the wide outdoors until school shut them inside again. In the winter when icy winds blew down from the mountains and snow covered the small houses and the fields, the children played closer to home, sliding on their home-made sleds, building forts and snowmen, while their mothers tried to keep the homes warm and winter clothing mended and dry for their families.

Summer brought other pleasures, too. Every summer Percy's Sunday school had an outing and he and his friends and all the families boarded the horse-drawn pleasure boat and rode down the canal to Llangollen.

While the parents visited, the older boys dared each other to leap from the boat to the tow path along the canal bank. And the younger boys tried to imitate them, eager to be thought big. Every year Percy or one of his friends was certain to land in the canal and have to be fished out by their fathers. But it was a great adventure, looked forward to all year long.

Parents sometimes complained about the strong odors from the Monsanto Chemical works on the edge of the village, but to Percy and his friends the chemical works were a part of Cefn Mawr, along with the mine and the fields and the canal and the mountains, and the smells were the smells of home—the best place in the whole world. Dominating the village at one end of the dirt street was the mine, where fathers and grandfathers and older brothers and uncles and cousins disappeared every morning to mine coal far below the sunny surface of their world.

Percy was vaguely aware of the gray cloud of anxiety that never quite left the village—anxiety that showed on the faces of the women and sounded in their voices. But it never really troubled him, for in his few years he had not seen a mine disaster. He had only heard about them.

Coal mining was all that men of Cefn Mawr knew. Boys in school bragged about the day when they would be 14 and could join the men working in the mines. Becoming a miner was the mark of manhood.

Sometimes when Percy watched his father come down the lane from the pit head, striding along with his friends; and when he heard their comradely laughter, broken by snatches of song in their deep, resonant Welsh voices, he thought that being a miner must be a wonderful thing indeed. He longed for the day when he too would be old enough to become one of them.

He discovered that his mother did not share his dreams. When he announced one day that he was going to go to work in the mines as soon as he was 14, she shocked him by saying vehemently "Never, Percy Davies. I want no more of my children down in that awful mine."

Percy stared at her. He had never thought there was any choice. All the boys went to work in the mine when they were 14. He started to protest, but the stern look on his mother's face stopped him. He knew better than to argue with her when she looked like that. But in his heart, he clung to his dream of going to work in the mine with the men.

Sundays were special in Cefn Mawr. Fathers and mothers and children dressed up in their best and went to church. Percy did not especially enjoy having to memorize the Bible verses, though it was fun when they competed against each other. And the singing and the preaching gave him the special feeling that they were in the presence of God, there in their little church.

The great Welsh revival had swept across Wales a few years before and many of the men of Cefn Mawr, including Percy's father, had been wonderfully transformed. These were the men and their families with whom Percy and his family worshipped.

One Sunday after the preacher had talked about repentance, Percy's father looked searchingly into the small boy's face, then took him by the hand and led him to the penitent form to pray. Percy prayed as he was instructed, but really did not understand either the need or the work of repentance. His life did not reflect any change.

There was probably good reason for Percy's father to take him to the front to pray, for though still very young, Percy had a violent temper that exploded when he was upset, sometimes with disastrous results. If his mother was near, she cooled him off quickly, picking him up bodily and pushing his head under the cold water tap.

"Percy! Percy!" she said many times. "I don't know what will become of you. Some day you will kill someone with that awful temper of yours, if you don't let the Lord take care of it."

When Percy was eight years old he was devastated by the death of his closest friend and playmate. It was the first time anyone he cared for deeply had died. He found it impossible to accept. Why should God take his very best friend? He resented the people he saw on the street going about their business as though nothing had happened, when his whole world was shattered. He grieved secretly for days, not talking about it, but hurting deep inside.

Tragically, only a few months later, Percy's father also became ill and died. This, added to the loss of his playmate, was more than Percy could bear. He could not cope with the awfulness of death. It was too monstrous.

Why were people born at all, if they must die? Why

am I here? he thought, sitting on a rock at the edge of the field where he had fled to get away from his other friends. Where did I come from anyhow? Will my mother die like Papa? Will I die someday? Where will I go when I die? The song they had sung at his father's funeral in their small kitchen repeated itself over and over in his mind:

A dear one in heaven thy heart yearns to see
At the beautiful gate may be watching for thee.
Then list to the note of this solemn refrain:
"Ye must be born again."

Born again! How? Percy knew it had something to do with going down to the penitent form and praying. But what was supposed to happen there? He had been there once. Nothing had happened to him. Maybe you were just supposed to start acting religious. He began to read his New Testament every morning before going to school. It was comforting to read from the Bible his father had given him.

With the main breadwinner of the family gone, it became very difficult to keep the home going. When they learned that a newer mine some miles away paid better wages than the mine in Cefn Mawr, Mama and the older boys decided they should move there.

The homes in the new village were newer and had more modern equipment than those in Cefn Mawr, but the miners were rough men who seemed to have been missed by the great revival. Their crude manners, their cursing and vile stories, their drinking made Percy's mother more determined than ever that Percy, at least, should not become one of them.

It was a cross to Percy. He was getting older and his friends with whom he played and went to school were dropping out to go and work in the mines. He begged his mother to let him join them, but she was adamant.

34

"Never!" she said firmly. "If you start, you'll never get out."

"Then can I go to work in the quarries?" Percy demanded petulantly.

"Perhaps. At least it's above ground," his mother said, surprising him.

"You mean you'd let me work in the quarries?" Percy asked.

"When you're old enough," she said. "I know that is hard and dangerous work too, but you'll be out in the sun and the fresh air. Maybe you can escape the terrible black lung disease that killed your grandfather and your father."

As soon as she allowed him to, Percy applied for work at the quarries. He came home whistling, proud to tell his mother that he was now a working man, and would be bringing home a paycheck each week. But it wasn't the same. Most of his friends were in the mines. He saw them coming home at night, already sharing in the close fellowship of the miners—the fellowship Percy had always longed to be a part of. In the quarries it was different.

On Sundays Percy's mother still saw to it that he went to church. Most of his friends went too. It was expected in good Welsh families. But during the week, Percy more and more did as he pleased. Most of the time he chose to join his friends somewhere to share drinks and talk. He never told his mother about his activities, but night after night when he came in in the early hours of the morning, he found his mother standing at the door waiting for him.

It irritated him to have her do this, and it bothered his conscience too, for he realized that she probably guessed what his activities were, and did not approve. But he did not stop, if for no other reason than to prove to her that he was a grown man now and could plan his own life.

Coming out of the house at 5:30 one beautiful September morning, Percy stopped for a moment to look at the beauty that surrounded him. The air was crisp and the trees were just beginning to show tinges of the brilliant color that was soon to come. He looked across the fields toward the mountains already blue with the haze of autumn. What a glorious day! he thought. Oh, to be a boy again and roam in the fields and forests all day long!

A man came hurrying past, his face grim and anxious —a startling contrast to the brightness of the new day.

"Good morning," Percy said, and was about to chide the man for his grim countenance when the man blurted,

"There's been a terrible explosion at the Gresford coal mine last night!"

He hurried on without stopping.

Percy was stunned. The day lost its brilliance. Hundreds of men and boys, many of them his personal friends, worked in that mine. How many of them were trapped underground there, somewhere beyond tons of fallen rock? How many would never see the light of day again? The terrible dread that haunted every family with fathers and brothers working in the mines was very real to Percy now.

Men were streaming past, hurrying to the pit head to volunteer for rescue service. They came from nearby collieries, from their homes, from everywhere, it seemed. Joining the stream of miners were the wives and mothers of the men below.

Percy followed, even though his brothers were not in that mine. When a disaster like this happened, you went to be of help if you could, or just to stand with those whose loved ones were below, letting your silent presence offer comfort to those who waited.

There was no possibility of a quick rescue. Some of these mines went down 3,000 feet or more below ground.

36

Horizontal tunnels branched off in many directions. The danger of further explosions was always there. The rescue teams had to proceed slowly, first making sure that deadly coal gas was not filling the tunnels through which they had to travel.

Percy stood with the gathering watchers, longing to be of help, but knowing his lack of experience in the mines barred him from even offering his services. The comradeship and close affinity of the miners and their families in this time of shared danger was like an invisible cord knitting volunteers and watchers together. Percy felt it, even as he realized he could not share it for he was not one of them. His childhood longing to be a miner flooded over him. To share in the courage of those who volunteered, to come home with them on the good days, striding along singing together, to have a mug of beer in the evening and banter together over jokes shared in the day's work—this to Percy, seemed the greatest thing life could offer.

Men from other parts of the mine not damaged by the explosion had already come up and were standing around the pit head when Percy reached the shaft. Volunteers with rescue equipment had gone down, risking their lives, to try to find any who were trapped, but still living. Half-running, stumbling and weeping in the early dawn the wives and mothers of those below were gathering to stand in vigil beside the mine entrance.

A few men were brought up on stretchers, or helped out by comrades, and a great cheer went up from the watchers as each one appeared at the top of the shaft. Not all came out alive. Some 15 stretchers came out bearing silent forms and were followed away from the scene by their weeping families.

The rescuers worked for days, trying to find any who might have survived. And the wives and mothers and sisters of those still below stood silently, never leaving the pit head, waiting, hoping that somehow at least one more would be found.

The last rescue teams to go down, came back to the surface empty-handed, faces black with coal dust, and etched with despair. They wept as they reported that they could not go any farther into the explosion area. Coal gas seeping through the shattered rock was ominous. It could explode again at any moment. It meant that it was very unlikely that anyone on the other side of the rockfall was still alive, and if by some miracle one might be, he probably could not survive until the area was cleared and made safe to enter.

Reluctantly the mine authorities announced to the waiting women and the men that hope for the 250 men below was gone. In order to protect the rest of the mine from explosions, they were going to have to seal off the area where the explosion had occurred.

Those remaining by the pit head turned and slowly began to walk toward their homes. It had happened in other years. It would happen again. They had hoped that the rescue teams could have reached them all and brought them out, living or dead, so they could at least know. But they understood. Other women's husbands and brothers had already risked their lives to go down and bring out those they had found. It was not right to ask them to take greater risks to bring out men who were already dead. But it would have been easier to bear if they just could have known for sure.

The scene of that pit head as the bereaved women and children sadly turned toward their empty homes, haunted Percy for days. It made his mother and sister even more vehement in their insistence that he was to stay out of the mines. But it only added strength to Percy's inner longing to be a part of that magnificent team of men who courageously faced possible death and never wavered.

That was manhood! Nothing else could measure up to it. But for his mother's sake, Percy stayed at the quarry.

When Percy was 21, his mother died. He had not expected it. It left him feeling terribly alone and defenseless. He had depended on her prayers to be a buffer between him and God's wrath. Now he felt exposed and helpless. Battling with his resentment at her death, he found himself again asking questions for which he had no answers. What was there in life to live for? What good did it do to be good? His father and mother had both been good and they were dead. He wanted to strike out at the ugliness of death, at the harshness and cruelty of life, at everything.

The uncertainty of the future tormented him. What was ahead if he continued living the way he was now? It was a downhill road to nowhere. His mother had died peaceful and serene. So had his father. They even seemed to welcome death. If what they believed was true, then they were together now, forever. But would he ever see them again? Not unless he changed, he realized, even though he tried to excuse himself.

In the midst of his brooding melancholy over his mother's death, Percy suddenly realized that there was nothing now to prevent him from going to work in the mine. He could join his friends at last. He could begin to share that close fellowship he had envied so long.

When Percy was hired at the colliery he was exuberant. He could scarcely wait to begin work.

But as the lift began to descend the shaft on his first day, his elation changed rapidly to anxiety and concern. He had not reckoned on the heat and dust and the total blackness below ground. He had not expected the terrible sense of being trapped as the cage, crowded with men, dropped lower and lower into the depths of the mine, one of the deepest in all of Europe. The cage opened and the men streamed out to their separate stations. The small tunnels visible under Percy's flickering miner's lamp seemed to close in on him as he followed the others. He was not prepared for the close atmosphere, the utter darkness that engulfed him. He set his teeth grimly, determined not to reveal his inner turmoil. Doggedly he did what he was told, longing for the day to end. About midday, just before stopping for lunch, he saw two men come past carrying another man on a stretcher. For one horrible moment he wanted to drop his tools and run after them, never to come down into this dreadful hole again. But he knew if he did he would have no friends, for they would all know he was a quitter.

The second day was no better than the first; nor was the third. He lived for the hour when his shift ended and he could climb on the lift and ride to the surface, to drink in the clean air and the sunshine and the cool breeze.

Sometimes he wondered if he would ever get used to it. Friends outside were no help. They looked at him in surprise when he told them he was a miner now. "Are you crazy?" they asked. "You had a job outside. Why did you go to the mine? Sooner or later it will get you. If not in an accident, then with the black lung."

He could not tell them why. He could not explain the longing that had so possessed him to be a part of that close-knit fraternity of men whom he had admired so long.

But the thought of death would not go away. What if I did die someday down there, he thought sometimes as he lay awake at night. Where would I go? He had gone to Sunday school and church all his life, but still the nagging fear persisted that this was not enough to get him to heaven.

In the midst of his inner conflict one Sunday morning his Sunday school teacher said to Percy, "What has Jesus Christ done for you?"

Percy could not think of an answer.

The teacher looked at him soberly and said, "Percy, you are not a Christian."

It was a shocking statement to be faced with, but Percy could not deny it. It was true.

Through the week the teacher's words kept coming back to him. I've gone through the motions of being a Christian, he thought, but it hasn't touched my heart. But he did not know what to do about it.

There were Christian men, even in this mine, he discovered. They were not hard to discover. They spoke openly of Christ and the Bible, and seemed not to mind if others made fun of them. Percy knew that if he had been in their place under the rough jeering, he would have shrivelled up inside. Nor were they cowards. Danger did not frighten them.

About a month after Percy had begun working in the mine one of the Christians was assigned to work with him. Percy braced himself for a hard time. But the man did not ask him any questions. He worked steadily and pleasantly beside him, and the difference between him and others with whom he had worked made a deep impression on Percy. After a while Percy ventured to ask him a few questions about the Bible and what he believed. The man knew more than some of the preachers Percy had heard. His explanations were simple and logical.

From childhood Percy had always said his prayers before going to bed. Now the Holy Spirit began to keep him awake. He was convinced that if anything happened to him in the night he would go to hell. Often he was on the verge of telling his work partner that he wanted to be a real Christian. Then he would remember his other friends; the ones with whom he had grown up and with whom he spent his evenings. He could not bear to let them go.

He worked all day in the mines beside his Christian

partner, convinced that being a Christian was the greatest thing in the world. But when his old friends asked him to go out with them at night, he always went, and joined in wholeheartedly. Then he would kneel beside his bed and groan over his sins, realizing that sin had him in its grip and he could not break away.

One day his friend in the mine gave him a book called *Christian Certainty*. Percy took it home, and on Sunday evening, December 20, he lay in bed reading the book and came to a sentence that said, "If you agree that you are a sinner and you are prepared to repent of your sins, then wherever you are, get on your knees and tell God about it. Now trust in the sacrifice and the blood of Jesus Christ and God will forgive you. Accept this forgiveness by faith and tell others what you have done."

"I'll do it!" Percy resolved.

"Wait until tomorrow," the devil said. "You have already said your prayers and you're cozy and warm in bed."

He jumped out of bed and knelt down in faith with no feelings whatsoever, and trusted Christ to save him. It was a matter-of-fact transaction. He followed the directions given in the book, trusted God, got back into bed and fell asleep.

The next morning at 5:30 walking to the mine, Percy met his work partner. Between the lamp room and the pit head Percy said, "I've settled the issue. From now on I'm going to be a Christian."

His partner's firm handshake said more than many words.

They got into the lift with the other men and on the way down Percy said, "I've settled it. I'm a Christian."

"You?" they said and laughed. "With your temper? You'll never make it, son."

"I'll give you three weeks," one said. "No more, and

42

probably not that long. You're not the sort for that life."

Before he had told many of his decision, one of them said "How do you know? You weren't a Christian yesterday. How do you know you're one today?"

"I believe God's Word," Percy answered. But he thought to himself, how do I know? I don't feel any different.

All through the day that was the question they threw at him, enjoying the discomfiture it created in his mind.

Their questions drove him to his Bible. He read it with a dictionary and Pilgrim's Progress beside him, hoping to find an answer that would corroborate the steps he had taken.

One night, walking home from the mine tired and hungry, the devil joined his tormentors. "How do you know you are a Christian?" he demanded. "You've always attended church and Sunday school. You've always said your prayers. In what way have you changed?"

Foolishly Percy began to argue with the devil. "Well, now I read my Bible and attend prayer meeting," he said lamely.

"And what makes you think that makes you a Christian?" the devil countered. "How do you know its any different? Do you feel any different? Do you look any different?"

Just then the Lord stepped in. His voice was as clear to Percy as though He were visibly there: "Him that cometh to me I will in no wise cast out!"

God had promised. He would keep His Word. A flood of joy swept over Percy in that moment of realization. His weariness vanished. He almost danced in his clogs down the street. He had never heard of the witness of the Spirit, but he knew that in that moment God had stamped His approval on his testimony.

When he went back to the mine in the morning he

testified again that he was a Christian. Again they demanded, "How do you know?"

And this time he answered with confidence ringing in his voice, "I know! Hallelujah!"

Now he was faced with the inevitableness of losing his friends—the men he had longed to be with—the men with whom he had shared evenings of drinking and gambling and bantering and a warm sense of belonging. As Percy prayed and agonized over breaking these ties of deep friendship, he decided that if he were going to walk with Jesus, his friends had to go. He continued to pray until he was sure that if he never had another friend in the world it would be worth it to walk alone, if he could just get to heaven.

How he would make the break with his old friends he was not sure, but he was determined to do it. Would he have to tell each one he no longer wanted to be friends? That was not true. He did want to be friends. He just didn't want to do the things they had always done together.

God solved the problem for him. A few days after Percy had reached his decision, his friends asked him to go with them to the Miners Welfare—the central hall in the village.

It will have to be tonight, he thought, bracing himself for the test.

As soon as they entered the hall, drinks were called for all around. Percy asked for lemonade! A chorus of laughter and joking remarks rose from his friends. Percy was amazed at the quiet strength he felt inside. A few days ago he could not have stood it to be the odd one in this group. Now it didn't matter.

Soon it was Percy's turn to pay for the drinks. As he sat at the table among his buddies he thought, "If beer isn't good for me, neither is it good for them." He got up, went up to the bartender to pay, and ordered blocks of chocolate for all the men, equal in cost to a round of drinks.

Some of them laughed, and some of them cursed, but for the most part they took it as a good joke at their expense. They parted as friends that night, but they never invited Percy to join them again for a night out.

Christmas was just ahead, and Christmas in a Welsh mining village was usually a jolly round of drinking parties entered into by the men with great enthusiasm. Already the invitations from many of the families had been received. These Percy had to sort out, declining those that he knew would be drinking and nothing else. He found it easier than he thought. In a village as small as this, news of the chocolate had traveled fast. They knew now that Percy really was a Christian.

It was the happiest Christmas Percy had ever known. He spent part of it with his Christian partner from the mine. His name was David, and their friendship had developed into so close a fellowship that they had earned the nickname of David and Jonathan. They walked to work together, they prayed and worshipped and studied God's Word together. And both grew stronger spiritually.

As they prayed together they became increasingly burdened for their village and the villages round about. They felt they must do something about the great spiritual needs. They began giving out tracts on salvation to every home in their village. They put up posters and gave out tracts at the gates to the field on Annual Rose Show day. They revisited the homes many times, leaving a tract each time and testifying to what God had done in their own lives.

That summer some students came to the little village church and preached on Perfect Love. This was something new to Percy. He recognized his own need for it, and longed to find this deeper relationship to God. He read every book and magazine he could get on holiness, and shared them with David. They bought copies of holiness magazines and distributed them from door to door. Several Christians asked for more. Between them they invited a team of men to come and hold a campaign in the village school hall that winter.

It was the second winter of World War II. German bomber squadrons droned overhead nightly on the way to bomb the Liverpool and Birkenhead docks. But people came out to the campaign meetings every night and many of them were converted and sanctified in the services. Percy was one of them.

A few bombs were dropped near the village, reminding the people of the certainty and possible suddenness of death. This may have contributed to their receptiveness to the messages.

When the meetings ended, there was a nucleus of believers in holiness, and the leader of the revival team, Maynard James, left a young pastor to shepherd the new group. He stayed only a few months before being called up to the armed services of his country, but it was enough to knit the group together.

Neither buildings nor building materials were available anywhere during those war years. The group of 15 adults and the Sunday school of 40 met in an old wooden hut without lights, heat, water, or sanitary facilities. And God met with them. It was a fellowship more close and warm and secure than Percy had ever known in the mines. He had not become friendless—instead he had found friendships that were richer and deeper than the best he had known in the mine.

On a summer afternoon the people of the village heard the sound of a plane overhead, somewhere above the clouds. It was not time for the usual squadrons heading for Liverpool. They went out of their houses to look, peering up toward the sound. Suddenly a plane dropped down below the cloud cover and came in low, heading for the mine head. There was no time to sound a warning. The villagers froze in horror as the plane droned swiftly toward its target. Suddenly billows of surplus steam burst from the boiler house and rolled over the mine head, completely hiding it from view. Seconds later there was a tremendous explosion in the field just outside the village. Clay and debris showered the mine buildings and the roofs of the houses. Men came running from the mine baths half-dressed to see what had been hit.

Through the Providence of God the cloud of steam must have momentarily blinded the bombardier, and his split-second hesitation caused him to drop the bombs harmlessly in the field instead of on his target. Had his bombs found their intended mark on the mine shafts, the winding machinery, boilers or fans, 400 or more men would have been buried alive that day.

It was a solemn day of thanksgiving in the village. Believers and non-believers alike gave thanks to God for His great providence.

The little group of holiness believers began to hold prayer meetings every morning at 7:30. Evenings after work they visited homes in their own or neighboring villages; they gave out holiness magazines, they held open-air meetings, and revival campaigns. They testified to everyone they could get to listen to them.

Their early morning prayer meetings, attended mostly by miners, continued for 25 years. Morning after morning the glory of God fell upon the group in the wooden shed. Men were converted. God moved among them. They had no pastor for five years during the war and afterward, but they carried on by themselves, with Percy as secretary, assigned to provide for the services and plans for outside activities. Much of Percy's free time was spent searching for a better building in which to worship. The land on which the little shed stood was not theirs and they had been told to find another place, for the owner wanted to clear the land for other construction.

Finances were extremely limited, but each Sunday they put away a little money for a building somewhere. There were surplus army huts available sometimes, but they could not find land on which to put one.

For three years they searched. During this time Percy earned his qualifications for a Mining Engineer and was assigned to lecture at the Mining College in a nearby town. While there, he negotiated in person at the Mining Offices and at last secured a 999-year lease on a tract of ground in his own village. With their small savings the holiness church purchased a prefabricated building and had it hauled to their location. Materials for remodeling it were almost non-existent, but as the seven o'clock prayer meeting brought their needs before God each morning, the money and materials trickled in just when they were needed. Volunteer workers came also, not all at once, but as site engineers, foundation workers, bricklayers, joiners, plasterers, and painters were needed, they showed up, two or three at a time, to do the work that was waiting to be done. For two years they worked summer evenings, Saturdays, and holidays. The final date was given them on which they would have to move from the old wooden shed. Step by step the work on the new church progressed, and on the date when they had to leave the old shed, they moved into the new church.

There were bills to be paid for materials, and there still was the need for securing a pastor and providing a home for him.

But they were in their sanctuary at last. Their faith was high for the rest.

All the houses in the village were either allocated only

to mine workers, or to the local council. No new houses had been built for years. There was a long waiting list of young couples who wanted a house.

What could the church do? They called a pastor, prayed hard, believed God, and began to build a manse. It did not come as miraculously as the church. They had to hire builders, and it took a year to complete the home. During this time their pastor, Rev. Clifford Filer, lived in another village and came on weekends to minister, until he and his family were finally able to move into the new manse.

One of the first persons to find Christ in the new holiness church was a young woman. Her whole family became Christians after seeing the change in her life. Percy saw the spiritual growth and insight of the young convert and was deeply impressed. They shared some of their concerns for the village, and gradually shared more and more common interests until Percy at length got up the courage to ask her to marry him.

They were married in the Welsh church, and continued to minister in the village.

Through the years the holiness group brought many changes to the rough mining village. Whole families accepted Christ through their witness. Rough miners became gentle fathers and husbands. Homes were transformed. Children grew up to become missionaries and preachers and strong witnessing laymen.

In the years after the war, the mines in that area closed. Percy's work took him and his family to Lancashire where he served as Education and Training Officer until he retired in 1978. But he did not retire from God's service. Even today in his home church he works in places of trust and responsibility and probably will until His Lord gives him a higher promotion.

GOD'S WOMAN

"Araxie, did you pray yet today?"

Araxie picked up her sweater and school books. "I forgot," she admitted, "But Papa prayed for us this morning. I'm late for school now."

"Go back to your room and pray," her mother said sternly. "Do not go out into the day without talking to God first."

Araxie obeyed. No child in the Guiragossian family would dare not obey when their parents spoke.

The Guiragossians were wealthy merchants living in Kesab, Syria, a large town on the border of Turkey. They came from a long line of prosperous merchants in Iran, and the descendants had fanned out over the Middle East, becoming wealthy and influential wherever they went.

In the home when Araxie was small, they had all the comforts that wealth provided in their country. Her Christian parents were both loving and strict. Disobedience was not tolerated. Attendance at church and Sunday school was expected. Every morning Father Guiragossian prayed for his family of five children, lifting up his hands to heaven like the patriarchs of old. The children went out feeling as though they had an umbrella of protection over them, for surely God would not dare to let any harm come to them after Father had prayed.

Growing up in this disciplined spiritual atmosphere, Araxie had many fears and questions as a young child. She did not dare express them aloud, fearing the ridicule of her brothers and sisters, and the possible disapproval of her parents. But she thought about them by herself. How could God be forever? Did He have no beginning? How did He create everything from nothing? Was God a stern disciplinarian waiting to punish those who did not obey His commands? Where was God? How could she find Him?

Often on moonlit nights, as a little girl of 9 and 10, she would slip outside and sit in the moonlight, looking up at the sky and wondering if God was up there somewhere just out of sight. A few times she climbed up on the roof of the house to see if she could feel closer to Him than she did on the ground. She went often to midweek meetings with her mother—the only child there. In one of those meetings she had a clear vision from God of the Rapture of the saints, though she had never heard anyone speak of this.

Sometimes it seemed that Satan also knew the spiritual capacity of small Araxie, for he seemed to single her out for special attention. One day as she walked home from her school in the valley to their home up on the mountainside, a great boulder broke loose up above and came bounding down the slope. Araxie was directly in its path, but she did not see it as she sauntered along, deep in her own thoughts.

"Run, Araxie! Run away!" people shouted. But they did not say which way to run, or why.

Araxie looked back at them, puzzled at their frantic shouts and kept on walking. Seconds after she passed, the boulder came crashing down on the spot where she had been.

While Araxie was still quite young her family met with business reverses, and her father lost everything he owned. They became very poor. It was an experience none of them quite knew how to handle. Their way of life was completely and drastically changed. It became a struggle just to keep food on the table. The high hopes they had built up for educating their children were destroyed. They could not afford even to send them away to complete their secondary school education.

But not once did Father or Mother Guiragossian blame God or question His goodness. Their faith more than anything else held the children steady in the new life of poverty with which they struggled.

Every year the village church held revival meetings. Often the evangelist was a pastor from Aleppo, Syria, not many miles south. When Araxie was 12 she gave her heart to God in the revival. This new relationship to God answered many of the questions and fears she had kept inside as a small child. She prayed publicly in the church services, and testified like the adults, to the surprise of her parents and the consternation of her playmates who would not have dared do anything so unusual as that.

She knew they thought she was strange. Satan tried to use them to trip the young Christian, reminding her that she would not have any friends if she persisted. But Araxie had heard the Lord's marching song and she walked ahead with a sure step.

She was a child of strong determination, a gift from God for her work in later years. Even while she completed the two years of secondary school offered in her home village, Araxie was planning ahead. Not for marriage and home life, but for a career of service. She wanted to be a nurse.

It was not a decision that pleased her mother. "Oh, Araxie," she exclaimed when Araxie started to talk about her plans. "Surely you can do better than that. That's a terrible life. I know we are poor now, but we have friends. Your father still has connections. Somewhere we can help you meet a wealthy young businessman and you can be married like other girls."

"I think this is God's will for me, Mother," Araxie said firmly. "I want to do it."

She did not speak of other directions she felt God had given her. They were too unusual—too extraordinary for anyone else to know. She kept them hidden away in her heart.

Very plainly God had spoken to her as she prayed one day: "Araxie, there are three things you must never do: Never get married. Never get a car. Never get property. These are my special commands to you. Trust Me. I will be with you as you obey Me."

Strange orders. She did not dare mention them to anyone for many years. But she knew with certainty that it was God who had spoken.

When Araxie had completed the two years of secondary school in the village she was determined somehow to get more education. She discovered that it was possible to get a student's loan in Beirut, Lebanon, and complete high school there if the borrower would agree to teach school afterward to pay back the loan.

With many misgivings Araxie's parents agreed that she could go.

When she finished high school she took a teaching position in a village an hour's walk from Beirut and walked to and from her school every day to save the price of bus and taxi fare.

When her school loan was paid, Araxie returned home

and taught school in her own village for a year. But she knew it was not for very long. Her dream of becoming a nurse was still strong. As she lived at home and saved her money, she wrote to the EMMS hospital in Nazareth. Because she had more schooling than many applicants she was chosen over some others, and while in training spent much of her in-service time working in the operating theater rather than in ward duty.

The Independence War of 1948 between Israel and the Arabs cut Araxie's training short. Because she was not Jewish, she fled with other non-Jews when Israel took control of their area. But she was determined not to be stopped. She studied the required books by herself, and in 1951 took the nursing board exams and passed them, much to the surprise of the examiners, who did not think such a thing was possible.

She secured a position in a hospital in Irbed, Jordan, and began at last the career she had dreamed of for many years.

While in Zerka one day, she learned that a baptismal service was going to be held for Christians at the River Jordan. How beautiful, she thought, to be baptized where Jesus was baptized! She asked permission to join the group. There were members from various denominations in the group, and the pastor who held the service was a Nazarene. It was the first time she had ever heard of such a church, and she was impressed with his message before the baptism.

Araxie's hospital work as well as her evangelistic activities sometimes took her to other cities of Jordan. Coming home one night very late from Zerka, she waited alone on a street corner for the bus. It was not safe for a woman to be out alone that late, she knew. She watched anxiously for the bus.

Three men came and stood at the same corner. Araxie

was not sure whether to be afraid, or relieved that she was not alone.

A car drove up and stopped. The three men spoke to the driver, then turned to Araxie and said "Come, let us go. Get into the car."

She was frightened, but did not know what to do. If the bus had broken down somewhere, there might not be another one until morning. She finally got into the car, and almost at once, felt an oppressive sense of danger. This is wrong, she thought. I must get out of here. But she did not want to beg them to let her out. If they were planning no evil, it would offend them. And if they were up to mischief, it would be better if they did not know she was frightened.

"Where is the bus?" she asked peering out the window of the car. "It should be here any minute. Where is it? I want to take the bus."

"Never mind the bus," the men said. "We'll take you."

I wonder if they are kidnapping me, she thought. O Lord, save me! Stop this car somehow and get me out of here.

They were close to the village of Mafrak when a truck came careening out of the darkness and sideswiped the car, tearing off the door. The car jolted sharply, spun sideways, and shuddered to a stop.

Araxie scrambled out quickly, ready to run or hide or do anything to escape.

The truck had stopped and the driver came back to see if anyone was hurt.

"Are you all right?" he asked.

"Yes," they answered, "but the car is wrecked. It can't be driven."

The truck driver glanced curiously at Araxie, wondering what she was doing alone with a car full of men so late at night. He started to turn away, and then stopped and stared at her. "Are you Mihran's sister?" he asked.

"Yes, sir," she said relieved. "Can you help me get to a telephone? I'm trying to get back to the hospital in Irbid where I work. I will ask them to send the ambulance driver for me."

"Get in the truck," he said. "I'll take you to the next village."

She scrambled up into the seat beside the driver. "Thank You, Lord," she breathed.

The driver gave the men a ride to the village also and let them all out at an inn, where Araxie was able to telephone the hospital.

The men were very subdued as they asked if they could ride to Irbid in the ambulance when it came.

Thinking about that frightening night, and other nights when she had had to wait alone for late busses, Araxie was perplexed. I wonder if I could have been wrong about that command not to get a car, she thought. Could that have been Satan, tricking me, so that he could keep me from my work?

She decided to try driving a car and see.

The first time she went out on the street she hit a man and broke his leg. He was in the hospital for months, and every day she had to see him as she went about her work.

"I'm sorry, Lord," she said. "I was wrong. I won't question You again. That was Your voice that told me not to get a car."

Araxie had more than one opportunity to marry during the years. Some of the men were wealthy, and could have given her the life of luxury and ease that her mother had dreamed she should have. But Araxie stood firm on the commands she felt God had given her: No marriage. No car. No property.

After nine years in Irbid, Araxie transferred to a hospital in Amman, Jordan, for two years. Then the government asked her to go to Aqaba to start a new hospital.

To her dismay she found no evangelical church there. She began to pray for God to send missionaries. It took a year, but they came and Araxie helped them start a Sunday school and church and worked with them for six years.

At the end of that time, she requested the officials to transfer her to the government hospital in Jericho. There were no churches of her own denomination in Jericho. As she considered which church at attend, she met the pastor of the Nazarene church in Old Jerusalem. On other occasions she had been in Jerusalem, and had seen the Nazarene church in the Old City inside the Jaffa Gate. She had met the missionary who was there. She decided to attend the Nazarene church in Old Jerusalem and see what the Nazarenes believed.

After a few weeks she realized she was getting solid spiritual food in these services, and in her decisive way she decided immediately to become a Nazarene. Often when the morning services were over at the Mount Zion church in the old city, she would go to the Nazarene Center for the afternoon service in English, led by the missionary or a visiting pastor.

Araxie was very much interested in the Nazarene preaching on holiness. Long before she heard of Nazarenes she had seen references to the sanctified life in the Bible and in Christian literature. Often she had prayed, "Lord help me to live a sanctified life. Teach me what a sanctified life should be."

But she was not sure just what this life was supposed to be, or how one achieved it.

There came a time when the preacher said in his morning sermon that all Christians should be sanctified "not just by name, but the inner man must be sanctified," he said. "One day we must face the Lord, and we must be ready."

"The inner man must be sanctified . . ." Araxie repeated to herself. Then it isn't just a holy way of living. It is me—inside me that I must be cleansed and made pure. Now I understand. Quietly, as she sat in her seat, Araxie committed herself to God and asked Him to cleanse and sanctify her life.

She became a faithful worker in the Nazarene Sunday school and vacation Bible school, while she continued as the matron of the hospital in Jericho.

When the Six Day War suddenly erupted in Palestine, the whole hospital staff in Jericho fled, except for Araxie. The hospital was full of patients and Araxie stayed on alone to care for them.

When the war ended she still remained, having earned the highest grading among all the nurses working on the West Bank.

The missionaries in Jerusalem moved to other responsibilities and other missionaries came to take their place. With a second couple in Nazareth, they began opening Sunday schools in the towns between Jerusalem and Nazareth, to the great joy of Araxie. She became the main leader in two of the schools, and then took charge of a third school in Ramallah on Friday afternoons which was the Arab Sabbath when they did not work and children were out of school.

Often she had to catch a taxi at the hospital and rush to the Sunday school, arriving just in time to begin. She spoke Arabic as fluently as she did English and her native Armenian, and her Sunday school lessons often became sermons as good as any theologian might preach, though she worked in a land which frowned on women in such places of leadership.

Though she had almost more than she could do already, God began to lay the town of Taybe on Araxie's heart. She knew very little about the town, but began to pray for an opening there for a Nazarene Sunday school. For weeks she kept her burden for Taybe to herself.

Then one day while attending the leaders' class in Jerusalem, conducted by the missionary, as they were deep in discussion of another subject, Araxie suddenly blurted out "Taybe! We must go to Taybe!"

The missionary respected Araxie's deep spiritual insights. He knew she was often led of the Lord into very definite assignments. He did not question that sense of direction now, but began to pray earnestly for God to open the door to Taybe.

Not all the workers were as faithful about coming to the class as Araxie. She came from Jericho every week and never missed a session. The others frequently came late, or forgot to come at all. One week, after waiting more than an hour for the others to come, distressed at their lack of interest, the missionary said, "Let's go to Taybe."

They set out in the missionary car wondering what might be awaiting them in Taybe, since Araxie was so burdened for the town.

They found a small chapel in Taybe owned by a widow who was a believer. Various groups had tried to start Sunday school or church there for years, but the people had broken up the benches, smashed a missionary car, and stoned those who came to hold services.

It was not a very encouraging prospect. Still the chapel was there. And God seemed to want the Nazarenes there.

"Would you let us use your chapel for a Sunday school?" the missionary asked the believer.

"Certainly, if you want to risk it," the widow said. "But you'll not find it easy."

"There has to be a reason God has put Taybe on our hearts," the missionary answered. "I'm ready to try it. What about you, Araxie?"

"Absolutely!" Araxie said. "All we asked God for was an open door. He's given it. We can trust Him to take care of the problems."

There were plenty of them. The first Friday (Arab Sabbath) they held the "Sunday" school they walked into pandemonium. Children were running around, yelling, adults were talking loudly among themselves. No one listened to the speaker at the front; no one sang the songs. It was total bedlam.

Exhausted they closed the chapel and started home.

"This is a tough spot," the missionaries said.

"Yes," Araxie agreed. "A terribly needy spot. It will take a lot of fasting and prayer to break Satan's hold on Taybe."

They covenanted to pray and fast for Taybe during the week, as they parted in Jerusalem.

The next Friday afternoon it was quieter. People seemed a little more aware of what they were supposed to do. Araxie's very presence, her assuring smile, her authoritative voice commanded their attention and respect. Within a few weeks as they continued to fast and pray for Taybe, a calm settled down on the meetings, and people seemed to realize they were in God's house.

"This is the first time in 20 years that services have been carried on here with any order," the widow said, marvelling.

But when the priests of the established churches realized that this evangelical Sabbath school was not going to collapse as others had, they began to take action. They threatened to expel every child from the village's only school, who continued to attend the Nazarene Sabbath school. Frightened by the prospect of losing their children's chance for an education, some parents took them out of the Nazarene Sabbath school. Children who dared to keep on coming were slapped and punished by the priests before their friends. The women who continued to come were excommunicated.

Under this kind of pressure the attendance dropped sharply.

"I wonder if we should keep on coming," the missionary said one day when the attendance was exceptionally low.

"Let's keep on a little longer," Araxie said. "I know God wants us here."

When the village school closed for the long vacation, the Nazarene Sabbath school suddenly was overflowing with children. Vacation Bible school spilled over into the outside. Mothers began to come back in increasing numbers.

There is still opposition, strong opposition. But the Sabbath school is there, and the people are responsive, and Taybe, the village so hostile, so unpromising, yet so heavy a burden on Araxie's heart, may yet become the most promising place in Judea for a new Church of the Nazarene.

One of the most surprising and disheartening things that met the missionaries when they came to the Holy Land was the oppressive and heavily depressing sense of evil that weighed upon them everywhere. It made every effort to start a Sabbath school or hold a preaching service a gigantic task. Demon possession was commonly spoken of and sometimes witnessed.

Araxie, who had become known among the evangelicals as a woman of great faith and prayer, was sometimes called by other churches to help them cast out the

61

demons from someone in one of their families.

Sometimes, even as the Christians were praying in the name of Jesus, the demon would seize his victim, tearing the person's clothes, smashing furniture, tossing bedding into the fire.

Yet after a prolonged struggle in prayer, pleading the blood of Christ, and commanding the demon in His name to leave the victim, he or she would be delivered.

Bethlehem especially seemed to be saturated with denomic forces. It was as though this birthplace of Jesus, once it rejected Him as the Messiah, was like a house swept and empty into which the demons had infiltrated with delight.

In one home in Bethlehem a woman had been possessed by a demon for several years. Her family asked the Christians to come and try to cast him out. They asked Araxie to come with them. As they united in concerted prayer in Jesus' name, they called for the demon to come out of her.

Araxie saw the woman's face begin to change into a horrible expression. It became noticeably darker and contorted. Suddenly she began to bark like a dog. Then a strange voice totally unlike her natural voice, spoke through her lips saying plaintively, "This woman can be saved, but I can never be saved. I will have to spend eternity in hell." Then the voice became strong and masterful and proclaimed triumphantly, "I am the leader of the armies of Gog and Magog! When the armies of the north come down, I will be their leader."

It was like the voice of doom—powerful, confident, authoritative.

It was a chilling experience for the Christians. If the demon was not lying, then satanic forces in the Holy Land were already gathering in preparation for the great final battle.

But in this instance he lost. Jesus Christ was still triumphant in the village where He had been born. As Araxie and the other Christians prayed boldly in the name of Jesus, calling upon Him to come, and pleading His blood shed for this woman, the demon struggled violently and left the woman, and she was restored sound and whole again. Later a demon claiming the same identity threw another woman to the ground saying, "You can't have her. She's my wife."

Satan's influence is strong in the Holy Land. Evangelicals meet with strong opposition. But doors are opening.

Araxie has found an opportunity to open a Sabbath school in Bethlehem. She has made contacts in Nablus and Zbabdeh on the West Bank. Workers are needed. Much prayer is needed. Believing prayer that can lock horns in battle against the opposition of satanic forces and open doors to the power of Christ and the witness of His servants in this desperately needy part of the world.

SOME THROUGH THE FIRE

Rumors swirled around the Christian school in Talas, Turkey: Christians were being massacred in Istanbul, in Ankara, in Konya, in Adana. Most of the students in the school were Armenian. They had grown up hearing tales of terrible purges inflicted on their people in years past. But this was now. This was today, and it was their families who were caught in the bloodbaths sweeping Turkey.

Hranoush Yardumian and her younger sister struggled to keep their minds on their studies. Surely, if the purges had reached Yazgad where Papa and Mama and little Edward lived, someone would have told them.

Papa was a leader. Papa was the church superintendent of the whole Yazgad district. If there were anyone the Turkish officials would want to destroy, it would be Papa. They prayed desperately that God through some miracle would spare their parents from the destruction that was decimating Turkey.

Hranoush was a senior. In a few months she would graduate. To what? What could any Armenian young person look forward to in these terrible days? She could only pray, and continue to study, hoping that it would be better soon.

Somehow Talas escaped the violence. It was like a small, peaceful oasis in the midst of the turmoil erupting all over Turkey. Indeed, all over the world, for World War I had been raging in Europe for two years. Turkey was allied with Germany. Britain and France were aligned with the United States. At first the war had seemed far away from the Christian school. But as the tide of victory began to swing in favor of the Allies, the British and French armies began to move steadily toward Turkey.

A spirit of hope rose among the students. What if the allies won? What if they conquered Turkey? Would the Armenian people be free? Would their nation be restored again, free and independent, a Christian nation?

The thought was exhilarating. Students and teachers followed the progress of the war closely, swayed between hope and fear as the battles were won or lost.

Spring came, and with it graduation time. Hranoush's mother came to attend her graduation, bringing Hranoush's little brother Edward. Papa could not come because of his church duties.

But before graduation day arrived, the Turkish army became concerned about the thousands of Armenians within their borders—unwilling aliens, who, they knew, would gladly support the enemy armies drawing steadily nearer.

They launched a monstrous purge of Armenian Christians. Thousands of families were sent away with nothing but the clothing they were wearing. Thousands were killed in their homes. Young men were drafted into the Turkish army. Young women were kidnapped and carried off to Turkish harems.

At the Christian School in Talas, students gathered in little groups sharing crumbs of news, worrying, wondering if their families had been caught in the purge.

65

The underground grapevine bristled with rumors. Refugees fleeing from city to city carried word of those arrested, deported, or killed.

One day the dreaded word came from Yazgad. Papa had been arrested, taken to some foul Turkish prison for no other reason than that he was a Christian.

Hranoush sobbed in her mother's arms as she heard. Good, kind Papa. Always helping those in need. Always teaching others to be Christian. Why Papa? Why had God not protected him?

Even as the wild thoughts rushed through her mind, she knew she shouldn't expect special protection for Papa more than others had. Thousands of Christians had died already in the purges. But Papa was head of the whole Yazgad district. Who would care for the churches now?

She shuddered as she thought of dear, good Papa being beaten and tortured to make him give up his faith. Papa wouldn't. She knew he wouldn't. And if he didn't he would probably be shot, or worse, driven into the desert with hundreds of others. They would probably never hear from him again.

Hranoush graduated from high school that summer of 1916. And in that same summer, the British and French armies redoubled their efforts to take Turkey. It was not safe for Armenians to travel. Hranoush's mother and brother stayed at the school.

In July orders came from the Turkish government that the girls' and boys' schools and the hospital buildings at the American Mission were to be turned over to the Turkish army for military use.

A few days later they heard the rumble of heavy motors and looked out to see a line of German trucks with German drivers, rolling up to the school doors. Students and teachers were marched from the classrooms to the trucks. No one was allowed to go to his room for anything.

As the trucks pulled away from the empty buildings, the girls huddled together with their teachers, too frightened to talk.

At the town of Cesaria they were ordered down from the trucks. Teachers and senior graduates were separated from the younger students and put into prison rooms with guards at the doors. For three days they were held in their damp, dingy, filthy cells. And for three days the officials told them that if they would accept the Moslem religion, they would be freed and allowed to work in schools and hospitals without fear. If not, they would be deported.

The women dropped to their knees in the dirt of their prison rooms and began to pray. Hranoush knelt with the others in an agony of fear, not so much for herself as for her sister and her little brother who had been separated from them. Where were they? What would become of them? She could only commit them to God, who, she knew, loved them, but even in His love, had allowed Papa to be arrested, and others to be killed.

The women rose united in their decision.

When the officials demanded to know their choice they said firmly, "We will be true and faithful and helpful to the government of Turkey in any way that we can. But as to our faith, we will be true to our God in heaven by all means. Jesus Christ is our Savior and Lord."

Angrily the officials went away. The next morning they herded the teachers and senior girls to a central area to join a group of widows of slain Christian leaders. Brusquely they were ordered to start walking.

Hranoush looked about her on all sides as they passed, hoping for a glimpse of her sister and brother, but there was no sign of them.

Poor little Edward, she thought. Only three years old. How frightened he must be! "Dear God! Be good to him," she whispered. "Keep him safe."

67

There was little talking in the frightened group as they trudged out of the town of Cesaria. Most were silently praying for God's mercy and deliverance.

They were led by their guards out of the town into the open country in the foothills of the mountains. Wooded ravines and rocky cliffs close by hid brigands who watched for defenseless travelers. Frequently they swooped down on Armenian refugees, stripping them of their few possessions and carrying off their young women.

Had any of these cutthroats attacked the band of helpless women, it is doubtful that the guards would have resisted. But God was watching over them and they were spared.

They had no idea where they were, or where they were going. They were completely at the mercy of the guards, dependent upon them for food and water and protection.

From the position of the sun and the direction they were walking, they guessed they were headed in the general direction of the Syrian desert, but it was hundreds of miles away.

That first day they walked until it was dark. The guards stopped them on a hillside in open country. Two of the guards went into the nearby village and came back with black bread and water for the hungry group. Then they were ordered to lie down where they were, and sleep.

There were no covers, nothing provided to lie on. They simply lay down on the grass, huddled together for warmth, and exhausted from fear and the long walk, they fell asleep. None knew whether she would see the light of another day.

Hranoush woke to the first streaks of light in the morning sky. For a moment she stared at the brightening sky above her in bewilderment. Then the events of the day before flooded over her. She prayed for protection, for a miracle of some kind that would deliver them from their terrible plight. But even as she prayed she was acutely aware that for thousands of Armenian Christians there had been no deliverance. They had gone to a martyr's death. The words of Job came to her with special urgency. "Though he slay me, yet will I trust in him." Yes, she thought. Yes, I will! I will trust God, even in death, if that is His will.

She felt calm and reassured as she rose and prepared for the new day.

Day after day they were led across the Turkish countryside, sometimes on dusty roads, sometimes through the low foothills and across open fields. It was all strange territory to them. The heat of the fierce summer sun beat down until some days they thought they would die under its rays. And other days it rained and the wind blew cold through their wet clothing. Yet none became ill.

As the weeks passed, Hranoush looked at her bedraggled dress and her scuffed shoes and wondered how long they would last. They had not had their clothes off since the day they were taken away from Talas. She began to look for signs that her clothing was wearing out, and realized, with amazement that shoes and clothing were still just as good as when they started on this long march. God was giving them a small miracle. Like the children of Israel in the desert, their clothing was not wearing out!

God has not forgotten us, she exulted. He knows where we are.

Weeks later, they saw ahead of them the distant outline of buildings against the sky. They were approaching a city of some size, and as the guards continued steadily in the same direction, they realized that this time they were going to enter the city, rather than passing by as they had all the others. Softly they speculated among themselves where this could be.

"Aintab!" the word came back in a whisper from the ones at the front. "It's Aintab. We heard the guards say it."

"Aintab!" How many miles had they walked across the Turkish countryside to reach this place, Hranoush wondered. And what was there about that name? Something—someone that Papa had talked about who lived there.

As if reading her thoughts her mother said softly, "There's a Christian mission in Aintab. Papa used to speak of it. It was founded by the revered Rev. Krikor."

Was this the end of their journey? Hranoush wondered. What would await them in this city? Would they become the pawns of some soldiers' barracks until death mercifully released them? Or would they simply pass on through, following the death trail to the desert?

The guards led the group silently into the city, past small shops, and into an area of homes. Darkness was beginning to settle over the city when the guards stopped, ordered Hranoush and her mother into one of the houses, and led the rest of the group on.

The house appeared to be empty. Grateful for a shelter from the open air, they shared the luxury of a bath, and a bed to sleep in.

Very early the next morning, Hranoush wakened, feeling urgently that she should get up. She rose, and heard her mother moving in the darkness. Without speaking, they dressed and silently made their way down the stairs to the street. It was deserted. They knew they would be conspicuous to anyone who might look out a window, but they felt compelled to leave the house. They walked along the empty street looking for mission buildings where they might find help.

They had gone only a short way when they heard hurried footsteps behind them.

Hranoush's heart almost stopped. Had the guards already discovered their escape?

Then a woman's voice spoke softly. "I'm a Christian Bible woman. Follow me."

They turned and walked quickly behind her to her home. Safely inside, with the curtains tightly drawn, she said "There is a rich man named Sarkis Negogosian who lives next door to the house where you were taken last night. He had a dream in the night in which there was a young girl. He was told in his dream to stretch out his helping hand to that girl. So strong was the dream that he was awakened and went to look out his window. He saw you walking on the street below. He feels sure you are the girl of whom he dreamed. He wants you to come to his house. We must go quickly before others are astir."

At first Mother Yardumian was hesitant. She preferred to find the Christian Mission and look for help there. But the Bible woman was insistent, and at last she consented to go.

They were welcomed graciously into the home of Mr. Negogosian.

"You are safe here," he said. "I work for the government. I am exempt from deportation because they need my skills. As long as you stay with me, you will not be touched. But there is no other place in this city where you would be safe. I need a teacher for my grandchildren who are here with me. I shall be most grateful if you would consent to teach them."

Once safely settled in the Negogosian home, Hranoush and her mother told their benefactor about Papa in prison and about their missing brother and sister.

"Refugees are passing through Aintab every day, from all over Turkey," he said. "If they have seen your family, we will hear about it."

On Sunday, Hranoush's mother asked hesitantly, "Would it be safe for us to go to church here in Aintab?"

"You will be safe if you go with me," Mr. Negogosian said.

He took them to the Christian mission, and in the congregation pointed out to them the family of the Christian leader, Krikor. "The old man is dead now," he said. "But his family is the mainstay of this congregation."

Though the deportation of Armenians continued throughout Turkey, Aintab was spared in the months that followed. Refugees, fleeing to the borders, streamed through the city. Eventually they brought word to Hranoush and her mother: "Your younger daughter is safe. She is working in an army hospital near Talas. Your little boy was adopted into a Moslem home."

Little Edward—to be brought up a Turkish Moslem! It was almost more than they could bear.

And not many days later came the news they had been dreading to hear—Papa was dead, killed because he would not give up his faith.

When the first bitter tears were over, a sense of relief crept into Hranoush's heart. Papa was free now. Safe in heaven. No more torture. He would never be deported into the Syrian desert now. And Papa had been true to his faith. Papa had won! He had not been defeated. She was glad. Her own faith lifted. It was true—God had not promised to deliver His children from all trouble. He had promised to give them grace to sustain them in the midst of trouble. And He had. Papa's triumphant death would give courage to thousands of other Christians who looked to him for guidance. Papa's ministry would last forever.

One morning Hranoush and her mother awoke to find the streets of Aintab filled with British soldiers. They had come at last! The news of the British occupation spread swiftly. Those who had fled began filtering back, eager to return home and begin life again.

But a year later, the League of Nations gave the mandate over Turkey to the French. Reluctantly, the British gave up their control and moved out just ahead of the entering French soldiers.

Close behind the allied occupation forces, American relief organizations came, opening orphanages for homeless Armenian children who were everywhere.

From the refugees coming into Aintab daily, they learned that their older brother in the Turkish army had been killed in the fighting.

And miraculously, eight years after he had been taken away, Edward was found. The Near East Relief Organization had gathered up all Armenian children from Moslem homes and orphanages. Edward had been given a Moslem name and taught to pray as Moslems do. They took him to a Christian orphanage in Aleppo, and then brought him to Aintab to his mother. He arrived, a frightened, hostile little boy, unable to speak Armenian, or to remember his mother and sister. He cried for many days for the adopted mother and home from which he had been taken so suddenly.

With security restored in the presence of the allied armies, Hranoush and her mother sent word to the younger sister in Talas to come to Aintab and join them. At last the broken, fragmented little family were together again.

With a family of four, Hranoush felt she must not impose on their benefactor longer. She went to the work center at the American Near East Relief office and said "I am a refugee. I would like to have a job."

The woman at the desk looked at her with a haggard face "I have heard many sad stories today," she said nervously. "I don't feel well. I just can't listen to any more. Please go away. Some other day I will call you."

"I don't have any sad stories to tell," Hranoush said gently.

But the woman did not look up again, and Hranoush left.

Two days later she got up courage to go to the boys' orphanage and try again. "I am an Armenian refugee," she said to the principal. "I am looking for any kind of work."

His eyes were kind as he said, "I'm sorry, but this is a boys' orphanage and all our help is male. Why don't you go to see Miss Kelly at the Near East Relief office?"

"I've already been there," Hranoush answered.

"Oh. Then you are the girl she is looking for," he exclaimed. "Wait here a minute. I'll have my chauffeur drive you over there."

"Oh, I'm so glad to find you!" Miss Kelly said when Hranoush came in. "Can you come to work tomorrow?"

Hranoush would have begun work that minute if Miss Kelly had asked.

She returned the next morning to begin teaching in the girls' orphanage. They were reasonably safe with the Americans and the French there in Aintab, they felt, but outside the city, things were far from settled.

World War I had officially ended with an Armistice signed on November 11, 1918, but the Turkish armies were not about to relinquish their nation to foreign control. As the armies of both the conquering and the conquered nations began to return to their homelands, the Turkish forces regrouped and began to battle with the French occupation forces in Turkey.

In many areas, the French forces were small, and totally inadequate to fight against a Turkish assault. In these areas, the French forces began to withdraw under cover of night. Often the Armenian families who had returned to their homes under protection of the French, first knew their protectors had left when Turkish soldiers smashed in their doors and massacred whole families.

Cities and villages were swept with a bloodbath as the French fled and the Turkish armies moved in.

Armenians in Aintab became frightened. Would they also be left at the mercy of the Turkish armies?

The French officers in the city were sympathetic. "We can't hold Turkey," they admitted, "but we plan to keep control in Syria and Lebanon. If your men will fight with us here, we'll do our best to get your families safely to Syria."

Every able-bodied boy and man in Aintab volunteered for training by the French, and joined with them to hold back the Turkish army.

In return the Armenian families flowed out of Aintab, in cattle cars furnished by the French, on donkey back, on foot.

The Near East Orphanage directors gathered their staff and the boys and girls and fled with the others, settling at last in Beirut, Lebanon.

The Turkish armies were on the outskirts of Aintab before the last of the refugees got away. And among the very last to leave the battered city were the Krikorians, parents of Samuel Krikorian, with his younger brother Pusant and the two youngest children, still at home. They reached Aleppo in September, 1919, and a year later traveled on to Beirut, Lebanon, and finally to Cyprus.

Hranoush Yardumian and her mother, sister, and brother went with the orphans to Beirut. There Hranoush taught school, and waited hopefully for peace, and a better day. They felt they were safe in Lebanon as long as the French remained in control. But the situation for the thousands of refugees pouring into Lebanon and Syria daily was tragic. Many came without money or posses-

75

sions, escaping only with their lives. They had been betrayed so many times that they trusted no one. And they found no welcome, for Lebanon could not absorb so many poor. They were hungry, sick, and homesick. They were emotionally distraught from the terror under which they had lived for so long. One person could scarcely do anything to help them, so vast and crushing were their needs.

Hranoush felt the best she could do was to try to save the children under her care and educate them to go out and earn a living.

She found a Christian church in Beirut, and in that haven, felt restored and refreshed as she worshipped God.

One morning in December, 1921, as Hranoush entered the church sanctuary she saw a stranger in the pulpit. He was a young Armenian, but with a prosperous look that was strangely out of place among the many poor who were in the service.

The stranger told them he was Samuel Krikorian, born in Aintab, the grandson of the great Krikor, the first Christian pastor in Aintab. A murmur of recognition went over the congregation, for many had heard of Krikor. The young man said he had fled to America, had become an American citizen, and God had called him back to minister to his people in Jerusalem. He was now on his way there to open a mission for the Church of the Nazarene.

Hranoush looked at the young stranger with respect. She could guess what it had cost him to give up his life in America to come back here into such overwhelming need. Truly, he must be a dedicated Christian.

He stayed in Beirut for a month, visiting with the refugees, listening to their stories of death and horror, trying to give words of comfort and encouragement, for it was all he had.

He left at last for Jerusalem and Hranoush wondered if she would ever see him again.

To her secret delight, Samuel Krikorian found it necessary to return to Beirut frequently to check on the refugees, and the homeless children in the orphanages. After two years of such visits, he asked Hranoush to marry him and share his work in Jerusalem.

They were married in March, 1924. In spite of all that she had seen and suffered, Hranoush was not prepared for the terrible destitution and suffering she found among her people in Jerusalem.

Unwanted by Jews or Arabs, the Armenians had taken refuge by the hundreds in the underground rooms at the Gregorian Convent. They were dark, damp catacombs, filled with old people and children. They were starving and penniless. They did not speak Arabic, and could not find work anywhere.

Samuel brought Hranoush to live in a large stone house outside the wall of the old city of Jerusalem in a new area.

As soon as they were settled, he sent for his parents and his brother Pusant. His brother Albert and the two younger children had been sent to America just before Samuel left.

They quickly fitted themselves into the household, taking over the time-consuming duties of getting food and water, to free Samuel and Hranoush for evangelism.

Now Hranoush was grateful to God for her experiences in Turkey. She found that the women would listen to her when they learned that she had suffered as they had. She understood their sorrows and heartaches in a way that Samuel did not, for she had endured the same.

While Samuel worked at planting the church, Hranoush spent her days visiting the women in the underground rooms. She conducted Bible studies and prayer meetings for them, and taught Sunday school classes for the children.

Pusant grew up and went back to Beirut to the American University. His parents went to be with him. A missionary couple, the Alvin Kauffmans, came to help Hranoush and Samuel with the church.

They were just beginning to get a good start when the Great Depression set in throughout the whole world. Money became increasingly scarce for missions. But with or without their salary check, the Krikorians kept on with their ministry.

Then World War II began in Europe. German U-boats began roaming the high seas. The Department of World Mission told the Kauffmans to come home for furlough while they could. Hranoush and Samuel were alone again to carry on the church. Through the war years, mail often failed to arrive, leaving them without any money for months at a time, but they held on.

When the war ended, throngs of refugee Jews began to pour into Palestine, fleeing persecution in Russia and Germany.

Every fresh arrival brought more resentment and violence from the Arabs. Terrorism became the weapon of both sides. The Armenian refugees were caught in the middle again, unwelcome by either group. Those who could, fled to America and Europe. In the hostilities that continually flared within Jerusalem, Hranoush and Samuel often could not leave their home for days at a time.

Aware that they needed help, the Department of World Mission sent a young British couple to assist them. The Russells arrived and began to study Arabic as they learned their way around. They were scarcely well settled when the Church asked Samuel and Hranoush to furlough to America in time for the 1948 General Assembly. They didn't want to leave, but felt they had to obey. They reached America in April, 1948. One month later, on May 14, 1948, Britain withdrew the last of her troops from

Palestine. And one minute after midnight, Israel declared herself a new nation.

Chaos broke loose in Palestine. Arab troops from neighboring countries moved in. The Jewish nation mobilized all their men between 17 and 45. The struggle for victory surged back and forth as cities changed hands half a dozen times.

The Armenian refugees were caught in the middle. They were not Jews and feared the enmity of the new Jewish nation. They were not Moslems, and feared the animosity of the Arabs. All who could, fled into the surrounding countries. Many could not escape and took refuge in the Gregorian Convent underground rooms where they lived in fear and want, afraid to go out for food.

In the midst of the destruction and terror, the Gregorian patriarch called for medical doctors to come and help those who were sick and dying in the underground. No one came. Finally after several months, Pusant, Samuel's brother, now a physician, came through the fighting and the bombing and stayed with them for several months.

When a cease-fire allowed the people to come out into the streets again, many of them fled from the city.

Then on July 8 the fighting broke out again, and this time the Israeli armies took city after city and held them. The Arabs fled from Israel, 652,000 of them. The Armenians fled with them. And the young missionary couple, frightened and alone, fled with the church.

Samuel had begun to apply for visas to return as soon as Israel declared her independence. For two years he was refused. Then he asked for a visa to Jordan and received it.

Samuel and Hranoush returned to find they owned a building in Israel and a congregation scattered in half a dozen cities in Jordan. They settled in Zerka and began to search for their church. They found a community of them in Amman and in Zerka and organized churches there. Others who lived in twos and threes in other cities were urged to start a congregation wherever they were. Within a few years, they had eight churches and missions with 111 members, and there were 400 children in Sunday schools and nearly 300 in day schools.

Their crying need was a Bible college to train pastors. After many pleas to headquarters, a grant finally came to establish a Bible college in Beirut, Lebanon, the most neutral country in the Middle East. It was completed in 1955.

The following year, the general church asked Samuel and Hranoush to come on furlough again. They had spent six difficult years building the church. They had lived through danger, political unrest, and uncertainty. But they had had years of wonderful fulfillment as they had seen the church planted in half a dozen or more cities in Jordan and Lebanon and a Bible college opened. Samuel was 63. He and Hranoush would rather have stayed in the Middle East until the Lord took them home. But they came to report as the board directed. For two years they traveled about America, speaking in churches, then retired in California. There Samuel took the pastorate of an Armenian church for several years, and continued in God's service until ill health took him home.

Hranoush continued to live in Los Angeles. Her children have settled nearby. Her bittersweet memories of the years in the Middle East seem long ago now, but the verse that she took for her own as a senior in high school when they began the long trek across Turkey, is still her promise and pledge: "Though he slay me, yet will I trust in him."